Meet the God Who Loves You

by
Camille Nehmsmann

Good News Ministries
Apollo, Pennsylvania

Meet the God Who Loves You
Camille Nehmsmann

Copyright © 1995

First printing 1995   *Second printing 1998*   *Revised 2001*

Unless otherwise noted Scripture quotations are from the *New International Version*. Copyright 1973,1978,1984, International Bible Society. Scripture quotations marked LB are from *The Living Bible*, copyright 1971, owned by assignment to Illinois Regional Bank N.A.Elmhurst, IL. Scripture quotations marked RSV are from *The Revised Standard Version*. Scripture quotations marked Amplified are from *The Amplified Bible*, copyright 1965 by Zondervan Publishing House. Scripture quotations marked KJV are from *The King James Version*.

All rights reserved. No portion of this book may be used without the written permission of the author. For further information, permission or additional copies address Camille Nehmsmann, Good News Ministries, 301 Young Drive, Apollo, PA 15613

Printed in the United States by:
Morris Publishing
3212 East Highway 30
Kearney, NE 68847
1-800-650-7888

Dedication

To my children Lou, Mike,
and Kathy,
and to my precious grandchildren

*I prayed for these children, and the
Lord has granted me what I asked of him.
So now I give them to the Lord.*
1 Samuel 1:27,28

Acknowledgments

My deepest thanks to:

My husband Lou, whose love, support, and provision are invaluable;

Joy Nehmsmann, my daughter-in-law by marriage, my daughter by choice, for her practical suggestions and proofreading skills;

Marilyn Keister and Barbara Evans for their friendship, prayers, and encouragement;

Joyce, Mary, Eva, Judy, Alice, and Pat, faithful friends and prayer partners;

Judie Schneider, whose encouragement has allowed this work to continue;

And especially to the Lord God Almighty, for His love, faithfulness, guidance, protection, and salvation.

Contents

Preface.. 7
Prologue.. 9
Chapter 1. Are You Here Only by Chance?........... 11
Chapter 2. A Loving Dad............................. 17
Chapter 3. The Divine Physician..................... 21
Chapter 4. Is Lasting Peace Possible?............... 27
Chapter 5. Protection in the Storm.................. 33
Chapter 6. Justice for All?.......................... 39
Chapter 7. Mercy!................................... 43
Chapter 8. Rescued and Redeemed.................. 47
Chapter 9. What About Life After Life?............. 53
Chapter 10. Project Restore......................... 59
Chapter 11. For Those Who are Successful.......... 65
Chapter 12. What is More Precious than Gold?..... 71

  Epilogue... 77
    Next Steps-Growing............................. 79
    The Manufacturer's Handbook.................. 83
    Becoming a New Creation....................... 91
  Promises from Scripture............................ 93
  About the Author................................... 95

Preface

The desire of my heart is that you will come to know the Lord more closely. My prayer is that this book will help you to do so.

I pray for you constantly, asking God...to give you wisdom to see clearly and really understand who Christ is and all that He has done for you. I pray that your hearts will be flooded with light so that you can see something of the future He has called you to share....I pray that you will begin to understand how incredibly great His power is to help those who believe in Him....I pray that Christ will be more and more at home in your hearts, living within you as you trust Him. May your roots go down deep into the soil of God's marvelous love, and may you be able to feel and understand...how long, how wide, how deep and how high His love really is, and to experience this love for yourselves...so at last you will be filled up with God Himself!
Ephesians 1:16-19; 3:17-19, LB

Prologue

We are all on a journey, searching for meaning to life. We've dipped into the pool labeled fulfillment and drawn out one promise after another, but all have failed to fill the void. Pleasure didn't satisfy for very long, nor did money, fame, success, or possessions. Just as a lock is made for a certain key, so we are made with a vacuum that can be filled only by a relationship with God.

Who do you think God is? Here are some views one might get from skeptics in response to that question:
"He created the world then went onto something else and left us on our own. He doesn't even know I exist."
"Is there a God?"
"He's this big dude up there with a fly swatter, just waiting to zap me if I do something wrong."
"He's a power-hungry egocentric Being who wants everyone to do things His way."

Why would anyone want to trust a God like that? Many of us have misconceptions about who the Lord really is, and therefore we tend to avoid

Him. Yet we all will meet Him face to face someday, so allow me to introduce you to Him.

Walk through these pages with me and meet my good friend, the living God, the One who loves you more than you could ever imagine. If you get to know Him as I do, your life will never be the same.

"The steadfast love of the Lord never ceases, His mercies never come to an end. They are new every morning; great is Thy faithfulness."
Lamentations 3:22,23 RSV

1
Are You Here Only by Chance?

Chance: To occur by accident; implies total absence of a governing mind, or a design or plan.

> "In the beginning God created the heavens and the earth." Genesis 1:1

The crowd watched in amazement as Air Force Thunderbird jets flew overhead in precise formation. We marveled at their skill as the pilots executed complex aerial maneuvers. During the air show the audience had opportunity to look over various aircraft on display, including a fighter jet similar to that used by the Thunderbirds.

A man standing next to me expressed admiration for the technology involved in building these planes. Suppose someone said to him, "Yes, and it all came about by mere chance. Minerals somehow appeared, and over time they randomly evolved into nuts and bolts, wires, gauges, and sheet metal. Other elements grew into tires, seats, and windshields. Eventually these parts just happened to come together to form this jet plane."

If the bystander chose to respond to this misinformed person, he would probably protest that this was a ridiculous statement. He'd perhaps assert that it took thousands of people, working over a number of years, to come up with a design, a plan, and then its implementation. He might talk about developing special metals, plastics, glass, electronics, and other products of highly skilled researchers who worked with a goal in mind.

In the same way, when I look at the order in the universe, and the intricacies of a human being, I have to conclude logically that these were made by a Creator with a plan. To my mind, it takes more faith to believe that random chance brought us and the galaxies and my beautiful roses into existence than to believe that a Divine Being with a purpose put it all together.

Just because we don't see Him, why do some conclude that God doesn't exist?

Our son Mike is an amateur astronomer and planned to bring his telescope to our home on a recent visit. I said, "Don't bother, Mike. It's cloudy and there are no stars out tonight." This young man likes accuracy even in casual speech, and immediately corrected me. "Mom, you know there are stars up there all the time, even during the day, and even if you can't see them."

I smiled at the gentle correction of something so obvious and thought, How like us. Often our view of the supernatural is louded, and we conclude that it doesn't exist or isn't significant in our daily existence. God wants to expand our vision and give us a new awareness of Him and His hand in our lives.

For those of you who are skeptics, would you allow for the possibility that this universe and everything in it was created with a divine plan and purpose?

"Our God formed the earth by his power and wisdom, and by his intelligence he hung the stars in space and stretched out the heavens. It is his voice that echoes in the thunder of the storm clouds. He causes mist to rise upon the earth; he sends the lightning and brings the rain, and from his treasuries he brings the wind."
Jeremiah 10:12,13, LB

I would like you to know, as I do, that you are an extremely valuable part of God's creation and very precious to Him.

"You [God] created my inmost being; you knit me together in my mother's womb. I praise you because I am fearfully and wonderfully made....All the days ordained for me were written in your book before one of them came to be." Psalm 139:13-16

God didn't just create you then leave you on your own, any more than I would give birth to a child and walk away, leaving him to fend for himself. Here is what the Bible says about the Lord's continuing protection and provision over those who allow Him into their lives:

"Jehovah Himself is caring for you! He is your defender. He protects you day and night. He keeps you from all evil, and preserves your life. He keeps His eye upon you as you come and go, and always guards you." Psalm 121: 5-8, LB

"One Individual life
may be of priceless value
to God's purposes,
and yours
might be that life."

Oswald Chambers

2
A Loving Dad

Father: A man who creates, originates, or founds something; one who exercises protecting care over others.

Create: The production of something new, rare and wonderful; the act of renovating, remodeling, or recovering something already in existence.

"And so God created man in His own image, in the image and likeness of God He created them; male and female He created them. And God blessed them....." Genesis 1:27,28, Amplified

"[The Lord]...is their shield, protecting them and guarding their pathway." Proverbs 2:7,8, LB

The story is told of a man renown for his artistry as a woodcarver. "How do you know what to carve?" an onlooker asked. "Look at this," the artist said, holding up a solid block of wood. "Can't you see it? Inside this piece of wood there is a beautiful bird just waiting to be set free. All I have to do is cut away part of the wood here and whittle a little there and pretty soon, there it is — a lovely bird!"

And so it is with God our Creator. He took a lump of clay and formed it into man, His highest creation. Then He stood back and said, "It is very good."[1] God looked down through time and saw you and all that you could become. He planned you ages ago, long before you took your first breath. You are so precious to Him that He gave His best and dearest for you.

Maybe you don't sense that. You may feel empty, unfulfilled, perhaps even a failure. Remember the second definition of creator? To take something already in existence and make it new again. God will do that for you if you will allow Him to. (Chapter 10 talks about the God who restores.)

God, as our loving Father, not only creates and restores, but His loving hand continually protects and guides us. I was reminded of that when the family gathered at our home recently. We had an unexpected Christmas snowstorm and were blessed to have the best sledding hill around. We could hardly wait until our two-year-old granddaughter awoke from her nap so we could introduce her to this winter treat.

Our Flexible Flyer sled was close to 50 years old, having been used by Jordyn's dad and granddad as well. While she slept, Jordyn's dad, Lou, took the sled down to Grandpa's workbench and carefully examined it under bright florescent lights, knowing his precious daughter would soon ride on it. His fingers moved over the sled's surface and found a splinter here, a raised nail there. He repaired every defect his careful check revealed, but he still wasn't finished. Before he would allow his child to ride on it, Lou himself took the sled down the slope and checked out the path to be sure it was safe, that there were no hidden rocks, branches, or other hazards waiting to cause harm.

When Jordyn awoke from her nap, eager Aunt Kathy, Uncle Mike, and grandparents urged her to take a sled ride. We knew she'd have a great time, but the little girl seemed less enthralled than we onlookers. Not wanting to disappoint the big people, yet somewhat timid, she ran to her father, locked her arms around his knees, and declared, "I go with Daddy!" Lou sat on the sled with his little girl securely in his arms, and they sped off down the hill together, enjoying every moment of the ride.

In the same way, God has a certain path for us to travel, which He knows will be for our benefit. But before He allows our journey to begin, our loving Father makes sure we are protected. He checks out the vehicle to be used (people or circumstances) and travels the path first before we even set foot on it.[2] The journey is not always easy; some paths are long and difficult. Yet if we allow it, God will take us in His arms and ride right along with us, feeling all the bumps, thrills, and chills, and He will see us safely to our destination. He has promised that He would never ever leave us or forsake us, that He would be with us always, even to the end of time.[3]

You can trust Him! God knows that at this very moment you are a work in progress. He lovingly watches over you and wants to give you the very best. Long ago He put in motion plans to bless you. He knows you by name and has written you on the palm of His hand.[4]

"I [God] have loved you with an everlasting love; therefore with loving-kindness I have drawn you and continued My faithfulness to you."
                    Jeremiah 31:3, Amplified

Endnotes

[1] Genesis 1:31
[2] Hebrews 4:15,16
[3] Hebrews 13:5b; Matthew 28:20
[4] Isaiah 49:16

3
The Divine Physician

Heal: To make whole, return to health; to set right again, to restore.

"I am the Lord that heals you." Exodus 15:26b

He was a leader, a man of authority accustomed to having his wishes carried out. But this was one problem he could not resolve, and it broke his heart. All his education and training, all his power and wealth, all the resources at his command could not bring his precious child back to health.

But he heard about a Man in another town who was reported to have healed many people with various afflictions. So the father set out to find this One who could restore his beloved daughter.

As expected, there were many patients waiting to be seen, but the Physician had compassion on this grieving father. He took several of His associates and went to the man's home to help the child. Within a very short time after the Healer's ministry, the little girl was up and walking and having something to eat. She was completely re-

restored! What a celebration there was in her home that day.

This true story can be found in Mark 5:22-43, which records how Jesus healed Jairus' daughter. But does God still heal today? Yes! The Bible says that Jesus Christ is the same yesterday, today and forever.[1] We have had the privilege of witnessing the Lord's divine intervention in sickness a number of times. What follows is one example.

Ken, a 42-year-old man, had coronary bypass surgery because his arteries were blocked. The blood vessels were so badly damaged over such a long portion that the surgeons at Johns Hopkins Hospital in Baltimore could only replace sections of what was clogged. They sent Ken home with the admonition to get his affairs in order because he had only six months to a year to live.

A small group of people from our church, including an associate pastor, went to Ken's home to pray with him for healing. We believe strongly in the biblical injunction that says:

"Is any one of you sick? He should call for the elders of the church to pray with him and anoint him with oil in the name of the Lord. And the prayer offered in faith will make the sick person well. The Lord will raise him up..."

James 5:14,15

When we arrived at his home, Ken was filling out an application for permanent disability benefits. His color was ashen, and he could walk only a few steps without stopping to catch his breath. Nevertheless we prayed in faith, believing God could and would heal this father of four young children.

Our faith was surely tested when Ken was rushed back to the hospital the next day, gravely ill. Yet we continued to pray and trust in God's promises for healing.

Imagine my surprise a few days later when I called to inquire about his health and Ken himself answered the phone. "I feel wonderful! I've just walked a mile!" he said. Apparently God healed him at the time of prayer, and his subsequent severe illness was a toxic reaction to the heart medications he was taking. Since he no longer needed them, they were poisoning his body. The physicians took him off all medicines, and he recovered quickly. Ken continued to make rapid progress, and was soon able to return to work. That episode happened about 15 years ago, and as far as I know, his heart still appears to be healthy.

The same Lord who cured that child two thousand years ago and Ken more recently can completely restore you to wholeness as well.

Whether you need physical, emotional, or spiritual healing, God is able and very willing to help you. I used to believe that God *could* do that but didn't think He *would* in this day and age.

I've since learned that when you become His child, He covenants with you to keep all the promises in His Word. He says simply to ask and you shall receive.[2]

Why not ask Him right now? Pray like this: "Dear Lord, please forgive my sins and restore my body, mind, soul, and spirit. Thank You, God. Amen"

Believe that He has begun a work in you because He loves you with an everlasting love.[3]

"If you abide in Me and My words abide in you, you will ask what you desire and it shall be done for you."   John 15:7, KJV

"The righteous cry out, and the Lord hears them; he delivers them from all their troubles. The Lord is close to the brokenhearted and saves those who are crushed in spirit."   Psalm 34:17,18

Endnotes

[1] Hebrews 13:8
[2] Luke 11:9.10
[3] Jeremiah 31:3

*The best things
in life
aren't things*

4
Is Lasting Peace Possible?

Peace: Inner contentment, tranquillity

"Peace I leave with you; my peace I give you. I do not give to you as the world gives. Do not let your hearts be troubled, and do not be afraid."
John 14:27

"Mike has a brain tumor and needs surgery immediately," the neurologist said. "We don't know what the outcome will be. Post-operative effects could range from mild disability to remaining in a vegetative state for life. Death is also a possibility."

When my dear friends Mike and Marilyn heard the grim news, a myriad of emotions engulfed them — disbelief, fear, anger, discouragement. It had been a disastrous 18 months for them even before this bad report. A beloved family member had attempted suicide and nearly died. Then their home in South Carolina was completely destroyed by Hurricane Hugo, and they lost most of their worldly possessions. When Mike and Marilyn moved back to Pennsylvania, they had the challenge of building a new home and acquiring all new furnishings to replace what was lost in the storm. Relocation necessitated new jobs for both of them, another big adjustment.

And now this terrifying word that Mike had a brain tumor. Surgery was scheduled, and when the operation was completed, his physician had further disheartening news. He said that he could remove only a portion of the tumor, since it was the size of a large plum. In order to prevent serious damage or death, the second portion needed to be removed after a few weeks of healing.

The stress of a second operation seemed overwhelming. Mike was in the hospital, being prepared for the second surgery that was to occur early the next morning. Marilyn was at home, pacing the floor, exhausted but unable to sleep all night. At 4:30 a.m. she fell to her knees and cried out to God. Looking up through the skylight into a starry sky, she said, "You have to help me, God. I can't take anymore."

As she bowed her head and wept, Marilyn felt strong loving arms around her, giving her a warm hug. Immediately all the burdens lifted, and she was flooded with peace. When she looked up, no one was there, but that feeling of the sweet presence of the Lord remained.

While very well aware of the reality of their circumstances, Marilyn seemed to be floating above all the turmoil. She went through the

Is Lasting Peace Possible? 29

motions of getting dressed, going to the hospital, waiting those hours during the operation. But there was such peace enveloping her that she fell sound asleep in the waiting room. This truly was that "peace that passes all understanding" that the Bible speaks of; it is beyond human comprehension or ability to conjure up.

When Mike came out of surgery, he waved, smiled, and said hoarsely, "May the Force be with you." Her husband was alive and able to speak and move! The Force is indeed with me, Marilyn thought, and His name is Jesus! Mike has since recovered nearly completely, with only a few minor side effects from the tumor.

Marilyn will be the first to tell you that while we are not always kept from every difficult circumstance, God will see us through if we but ask Him. She knows that divine peace is real, and that any child of God who calls upon the Lord can experience it.

What challenges are you facing today? Does your job have you in turmoil? Is the stress of a broken relationship, physical illness, financial burdens or feelings of loneliness and emptiness overwhelming to you? Why not ask God to give you His peace right now? The Lord Himself says in His Word:

"Don't worry about anything; instead, pray about everything; tell God your needs and don't

forget to thank Him for His answers. If you do this you will experience God's peace, which is far more wonderful than the human mind can understand. His peace will keep your thoughts and your hearts quiet and at rest as you trust in Christ Jesus."

Philippians 4:6,7, LB

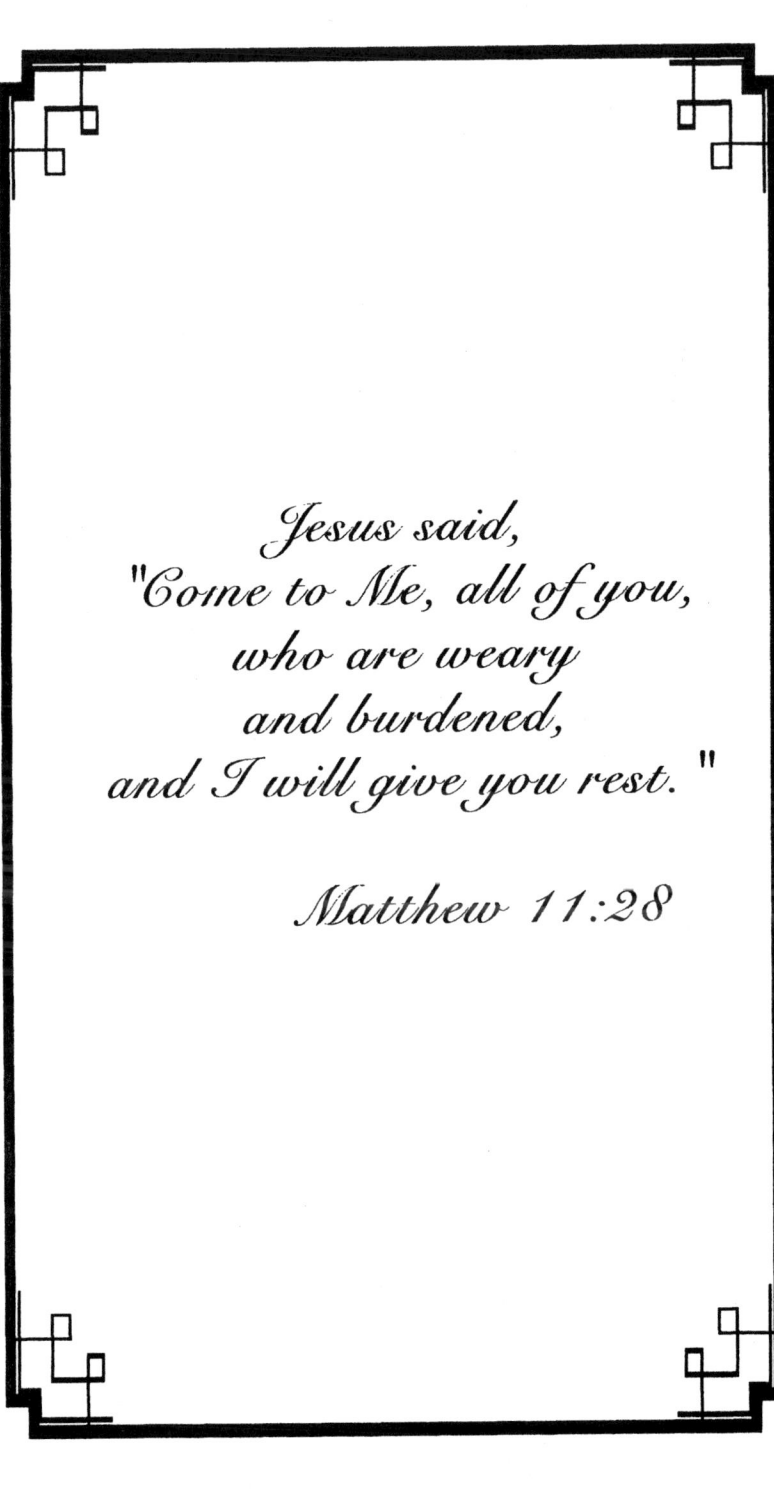

5
Protection in the Storm

Protect: To keep from being damaged, attacked, stolen, or injured.

"He [God] will command his angels concernng you, to guard you in all your ways...."Because he loves me," says the Lord, "I will rescue him; I will protect him, for he acknowledges my name. He will call upon me, and I will answer him; I will be with him in trouble, I will deliver him and honor him. With long life I will satisfy him, and show him my salvation."
Psalm 91:11, 14-16

Nora Lam stood before a firing squad blindfolded, with hands tied behind her back. She could scarcely believe that this was happening to her. "Ready! Aim!" The reality of impending death engulfed her.

Nora was born in China in the 1930s, the daughter of a respected and prosperous physician. She had a relationship with Christ as a child but became distant from Him in young adulthood. Life was good for her and her family at first, but when the Japanese attacked China in World War II, they underwent terrible tribulation. Things became even worse when the Communists took over her country in the late 1940s.

Nora obtained a law degree and married a fellow student. Required to teach in a Communist school, she was harassed daily. Despite the fact that Nora was obviously pregnant, she was slapped and punched, even knocked unconscious once during a period of intense questioning by the communists.

On one occasion when Nora was subject to interrogation by atheistic party officials, she was challenged about her earlier years as a Christian. Although she had not been in communion with Jesus for quite awhile, the interrogators challenged her earlier beliefs and commanded that she deny Christianity. Something rose up within her, a remembrance of her earlier faith. "Jesus may be distant from me, but I will not deny his existence.... Yes, I am a Christian."[1] Her interrogator shook with rage and shouted, "Take her out and shoot her!"

She was escorted out to a courtyard and stood before the firing squad. "Ready!" someone shouted, and she could hear the rifle bolts click. "Aim!" She whispered the words of Psalm 23, "Though I walk through the valley of the shadow of death, I shall fear no evil for thou art with me."

Nora asked God to forgive her sins and take care of her family. "Fire!" Guns exploded, bullets cracked, and she felt the sting of chips of brick as armor pierced the wall behind her.

She tells us that "I collapsed onto the ground. Was this all there was to dying? Then I realized that I was still breathing. I was still alive. What had happened?" Her blindfold was removed, and she saw the firing squad staring at her, seemingly in shock, their rifles lowered. She was taken back into the building to talk to another interrogator. "I felt the light, the warmth...bullets struck all around me," Nora told him, still amazed that she was alive. He replied, "It has been determined that it was some form of electrical disturbance. A freak windstorm." He tried to explain away why this pregnant young woman did not die when trained marksmen shot directly at her.

Nora continued to have many difficult experiences in China but eventually was allowed to come to America with her children. She established a ministry with the goal of bringing the Gospel message to China. Many have been led to Christ through this outreach. Years later a friend told her a story related by a fellow student at Stanford University. This friend happened to be seated next to a man from mainland China and asked him for his testimony about how he became a Christian. This is what he said:

"I was a sharpshooter in Communist China, assigned to a firing squad. One day a woman was brought before us who admitted to being a Christian. She wouldn't deny her God but prayed aloud to him during the last three minutes she had to live.

"We tried three times to shoot her, but each time we heard the count to fire, a brilliant light came down from the sky, blinding us. Our guns became almost too hot to hold, and as we squeezed the triggers, the guns were jerked upwards by some unseen force. This happened three times.... I dropped my gun and ran, taking refuge in a Catholic convent.... I wanted to know the kind of God that woman knew, that God with real power. There in the convent I met Jesus."

The Lord of power and might who rescued Nora Lam will also protect you, if you but call upon Him. He has a purpose for your life and will preserve you from harm because He loves you and so that you might fulfill His plan for you.

"He holds victory in store for the upright, he is a shield for those whose walk is blameless, for he guards the course of the just and protects the way of his faithful ones."   Proverbs 2:7,8

---

[1] Nora Lam and Richard Schneider, *China Cry: The Nora Lam Story*, Thomas Nelson Pub- lishers, Nashville, TN: 1991; p. 128, 238.

*Life is a series
of wonderful opportunities,
brilliantly disguised
as impossible situations.*

Charles Swindoll

6
Justice for All?

Just: Honorable and fair in one's dealings and actions. Consistent with what is morally right; righteous. Properly due or merited.

> *"All have sinned and come short of the glory of God."* Romans 3:23
> *"[God] will not leave the guilty unpunished."* Nahum 1:3

I grew up thinking that God was a stern judge, just waiting for me to sin so that He could strike me dead and cast me into hell. I've since come to see how wrong I was, how very much God loves me. I've learned of all the provisions He's made so that I could be saved. In discussing God's justice, these principles need to be kept in mind:

- Man was created for fellowship with God, but sin separated us from Him. He gave us free will so that we could choose to love and serve Him, or to do it "our way."

- Sin is disobedience to God's law, and a just God cannot overlook our transgressions. Just as one must be punished in our society for breaking the law, so too there is a penalty to be paid for sin. It will cause us to spend eternity in hell if we do not repent.

- God has made a way to rescue us from the penalty for sin, and that is through the death and resurrection of Jesus Christ.

As a parent, I've experienced that love for a child that will prompt me to do anything to save him, even to giving up my own life. Since I love my children so much, there are certain behaviors that cannot be permitted because these are so destructive to their well-being. If a little one runs into the street, or plays with fire, he must be stopped. Rules have been set in place, and when those regulations are violated, punishment must follow. Rather than waiting for them to err so I can zap them, I grieve when my children transgress and have to be punished.

The love I have for my children is only a fraction of the love Father God has for us. *He will do anything except violate our free will in order to save us.* He has set rules in place for our good, to keep us healthy and happy. He knows how destructive such things as lying, adultery, and stealing are to us and those around us, and God must prohibit such behavior. Yet it breaks His heart to see us transgress. He makes repentance as easy as saying, "I'm sorry; forgive me."

Read on to learn more about the God of mercy and about Jesus our Redeemer, who actually did give His life so we could be saved for eternity.

"If we confess our sins, he is faithful and just and will forgive us our sins and purify us from all unrighteousness."

1 John 1:9

7
Mercy!

Mercy: Kind and compassionate treatment of an offender; a disposition to be kind and forgiving; alleviation of distress, clemency.

"The steadfast love of the Lord never ceases, His mercies never come to an end; they are new every morning; great is Thy faithfulness."
Lamentations 3:22,23, RSV

"Les Miserables" was written by Victor Hugo and set during the French Revolution. It tells the story of Jean Valjean, who was sentenced to 19 years of hard labor because he stole food to feed his sister's hungry children. When he was finally released, he had become an impoverished, bitter man. The bishop of Digne was the only one who treated him kindly, inviting Valjean into his home. Not only was this gesture of benevolence not appreciated, but Valjean stole the bishop's silver as well. He was caught by the police and taken to the bishop's house before going to prison.

To the thief's astonishment, the bishop covered his crime, telling police the silver was a gift, and then giving Valjean that silver and two valuable candlesticks as well. This act of mercy not only negated the prison sentence in store for the criminal, but changed him completely. His life from then on became an example of compassion and kindness.

In the same way, God shows compassion on us when we repent of our sins. God loves us so much that He desires that no one should go to hell.[1] Therefore He sent His Son Jesus to take our just punishment upon Himself, so we could be redeemed. All we have to do is ask. (See the chapter on salvation, chapter 9.)

There is a debt we can never repay. In His mercy and loving kindness the Lord not only covers our sins, but washes them away, as if they never existed. He says, "I will forgive their wickedness and remember their sins no more."[2]

The story is also told of a young man who persuaded his father to give him his inheritance and then left home and squandered the money on a life of wild parties. When the money was gone, so were his newfound friends. The wayward man soon found himself homeless and hungry. After living in squalor and deprivation for a while, he came to his senses and decided to go back to Dad and ask if he could become a hired hand on the family farm.

When the father saw his son approaching, did he think, "Ha! He got just what he deserved. Boy, is he in for a surprise if he thinks he's going to get any more out of me. I'll let him know just what I think of his foolishness."

That did *not* happen. In his love and mercy, the father ran out to meet his boy, threw his arms around him and gave him a big hug. He invited all the family and friends to a sumptuous "welcome home" party for his child who had returned. This story of the prodigal son is found in Luke 15:11-24.

Our heavenly Father waits with open arms to receive us, to restore the broken relationship, and to help us begin a new life. Jesus said that if anyone came to Him, He would certainly not turn him away.[3] Just as the prodigal son had a party given for him, there is a huge celebration in heaven when we come to the Lord, or return after having left Him. There is a crowd of angels and saints rooting for us to succeed.[4]

"He [God] is patient with you, not wanting anyone to perish, but everyone to come to repentance." 2 Peter 3:9

Endnotes

[1] 2 Peter 3:9
[2] Jeremiah 31:34b
[3] John 6:37
[4] Hebrews 12:1

8
Rescued and Redeemed

Redeem: To recover ownership by paying a specified sum; to set free, to rescue or ransom; to save from a state of sinfulness and its consequences.

"He has rescued us out of the darkness and gloom of Satan's kingdom and brought us into the kingdom of His dear Son, who bought our freedom with His blood and forgave us all our sins."
                          Colossians 1:13,14 , LB

There once was a king whose servants informed him that someone was stealing things from the castle. Outraged, the king demanded that the thief be caught and punished by 39 lashes. One day his servants came to him and said they had found the criminal. "Bring the thief here, and call in the guards with their whip," the king ordered. "Punishment must be given here and now." Imagine his astonishment when they brought forth the culprit, and it turned out to be the king's daughter, whom he loved with all his heart.

What to do? The penalty had to be paid.

Without a moment's hesitation the king took off his royal robes, bared his back, and said to those executing the beating, "Take me instead, and let her go free."

That's exactly what Jesus the Redeemer did for us. He put aside His royal robes, came to earth and was crucified, punished in our place, so that we might escape the penalty for sin. The price has already been paid for our transgressions. Our part is to receive what has been given.

Let us suppose that I went on a three day trip, but before leaving stocked the freezer with three full days of nutritious meals for the family members who remained at home. What if I arrived home to hear them say, "Thank goodness you are back. We haven't had a decent meal in ages." I had made provision for them, but their part was to take and use what was already prepared. The work was done, the price paid. They simply had to take what was willingly given.

Likewise, we must take the salvation Jesus offers to us. The cost has already been met, and we have only to claim the blessing. But we are responsible for taking that step of accepting Christ into our lives. Just as I could not force my family to eat the meals prepared, so also *Jesus will not force Himself into our lives. In His infinite love, He gave us free will. The choice is ours.* Will you allow His presence and peace to fill your hungry heart? Read on to see how you can do exactly that.

"Jesus told him, 'I am the Way — yes, and the Truth and the Life. No one can get to the Father except by means of Me.' " John 14:6, LB

[Jesus said] "Look! I have been standing at the door and I am constantly knocking. If anyone hears Me calling him and opens the door, I will come in and fellowship with him and he with Me." Revelation 3:20, LB

"It wasn't nails that kept
Christ on the cross.
It was love."

Max Lucado

9
What About Life After Life?

Salvation: Preservation or deliverance from destruction, difficulty, or evil. Deliverance from the power or penalty of sin; redemption. The agent or means that brings about such deliverance.

'If you confess with your mouth 'Jesus is Lord,' and believe in your heart that God raised Him from the dead, you will be saved.'
Romans 10:9

They fastened their seat belts, prepared for an uneventful landing. Many were business travelers, "frequent fliers," and this trip to Pittsburgh on Flight 427 seemed just like any other. It was a clear sunny afternoon in September when suddenly, without warning, the aircraft rolled on its side and plunged to earth. Within seconds, everyone on board was killed.

As we read vivid details about the crash and its victims, we were reminded once again how fragile life is and how quickly it can end. Our thoughts turned to loved ones and their spiritual readiness to go into eternity. We pondered about why some have not chosen to walk with Christ.

You may be one of the many who have said, "I believe in God, but I don't want to make a commitment yet. I want to enjoy life first. I'll think about God later, when I'm older. I have plenty of time." Later never came for those airline passengers.

Maybe you have had a bad experience with religion or church people. We are not talking about a religion or denomination but a relationship with God, a personal daily walk with Christ. Don't evaluate Him by the actions of people. Humans make mistakes and have feet of clay, but God the Almighty loves you unconditionally. He wants only the best for you and has the power to accomplish that if you will allow Him to.

Perhaps you have said, "I'm a good person. Jesus wouldn't send me to hell." God has said that there is only one way to heaven — by repenting of your sins and asking Jesus Christ into your heart. His Word says, "All have sinned and fall short of the glory of God" (Romans 3:23). *Your salvation is not based on performance; there is nothing you can do to earn it by your own works. It is a gift of grace, based solely on a personal relationship with Jesus Christ.* (See Ephesians 2:8,9.)

Conversely, some think they have done too many bad things and have to "get their act together" before approaching God. One of the beautiful things about His unconditional love is that the Lord will take you right where you are and work with you in that place. If my son handed me his little girl who needed a bath, I wouldn't say, "Clean her up first or I won't take her." It would be such a joy just to have her in my arms, whatever her condition, and that's how God feels about you.

Possibly your mind cannot comprehend all the aspects of God, or the mystery of salvation. I do not fully understand how a computer works, nor all the math and electronics involved. But I have no hesitation in using it to benefit me for word processing, graphics, and a myriad of other things. I turn on the switch and use what has been provided. In the same way you can simply come to God and tell Him you don't comprehend all there is to know about Him, but that if what you've read here is true, you want the benefits of life with Him.

You've read in these pages all the good things God wants to bestow upon us because He loves us. We've said that He is also a God of justice, and as such, cannot let sin go unpunished. We've talked about His mercy, and that Jesus our Redeemer has already paid the price for our sins.

Please carefully think about all that has been written here, and seriously consider asking Jesus into your heart. The way to do so is to simply admit that you have sinned, ask God to forgive you, and invite Jesus to be your Lord and Savior. What have you got to lose?

When you accept Jesus into your heart, you enter into a covenant with Him and are a recipient of all the promises He has made in the Bible. You are assured of eternal life with Him in heaven, as well as manifold blessings upon this earth.

To begin this new life in Christ you can say this prayer or a similar one in your own words:

Lord Jesus Christ, I admit that I am a sinner, and that You died and rose again to redeem me from my sins. Please forgive me. Come into my heart and be my Lord and Savior. Thank You, God, that You have heard my prayer and I am now in Your kingdom. Help me to live the life You have chosen for me. Amen!

If you said that prayer with your heart, Jesus assures you that you are saved from hell and can look forward to eternity in heaven as well as abundant life here on earth. Welcome to life in a new dimension!

"I say emphatically that anyone who listens to My message and believes in God who sent Me has eternal life, and will never be damned for his sins, but already has passed out of death into life."
John 5:24, LB

Written by a Soldier in Vietnam

Lord, I've never spoken to You,
But now I want to say, "How do You do."
You see, God, they told me You didn't exist,
And like a fool, I believed all of this.

Last night from a foxhole I saw Your sky.
I figured right then they'd told me a lie.
Had I taken the time to see the things
    You made,
I'd have known they weren't calling a spade
    a spade.

I wonder, God, if You'll take my hand.
Somehow I feel that You'll understand.
Funny how I had to come to this hellish place
Before I came to see Your face.

Well, I guess there isn't much more to say
But I'm sure glad I met You today.
I guess zero hour will soon be here,
But I'm not afraid since I know You're near.

The signal. Well, God, I'll have to go.
I love You lots, I want You to know.
Now this will be a horrible fight.
Who knows? I may come to Your house tonight.

Though I wasn't friendly to You before,
I wonder, God, if You'd wait at the door.
Look, I'm crying. Me, shedding tears.
I wish I'd known You these many years.
Well, I have to go now, God. Good-bye.
Strange, since I met You I'm not afraid to die.

(This poem was found on his body at the battlefront and sent to his mother).

Author Unknown

10
Project Restore

Restoration: To bring back to a previous normal condition; to be reinstated, reconstructed, renovated.

"I have seen his ways, but I will heal him; I will guide him and restore comfort to him."
Isaiah 57:18

The battered old desk certainly showed the scars of being 150 years old. I had inherited the Victorian walnut piece of furniture from my parents and wondered if it could ever be restored. All I saw were the ink stains, water marks, gouges, and charred places where candles had been left to burn too long some hundred years ago. It looked like a hopeless mess to me.

But my husband, Lou, saw what it could become. He said, "Look at these classic lines and that beautiful burled veneer. This brass is the original hardware." Carefully, lovingly, skillfully, he made new parts only where needed and refinished the rest. Step by step he removed years of accumulated dirt and varnish, gently sanded and filled deep scars, then stained, varnished and waxed the desk. When this craftsman finished his work, the furniture was beautiful to behold and is now a treasured family heirloom.

In the same way, Jesus comes to restore our lives. He doesn't destroy the essence of what we are but only works on those things that mar our beauty. He carefully works in us over a period of time, investing patience, love and skill, because He sees us not as we are but as the masterpiece we will become. Let Him do a work in your heart and help you to be all you were made to be!

Perhaps you knew the Lord once, and walked closely with Him, but have since turned and gone your own way. The God of restoration waits with outstretched arms to receive you back again.

This poem by Myra Brooks Welsch,"The Touch of the Master's Hand," illustrates how Christ can take something considered worthless and make it into something of infinite value.

The story begins with an auctioneer selling an old violin. He holds it up and says, "What am I bid for this old violin? $1? $2? Who'll make it $3?" Just before the old violin was sold for $3, a gray-haired old man came forward, took the violin and bow, and dusted them off. He tightened the strings and began to play beautiful music.

After that the auctioneer held the violin up and said, "What am I bid? $2,000? $3,000?" The poem concludes this way:

"The people cheered, but some of them cried,
We do not quite understand

What changed its worth. Swift came the reply:
The touch of a master's hand.

And many a man with a life out of tune,
And battered and scarred with sin,
Is auctioned off cheap to the thoughtless crowd,
Much like the old violin.

A mess of pottage, a glass of wine, a game –
And he travels on.
He's "going once, going twice;"
He's "going" and almost "gone."

But the Master comes and the foolish crowd
Never can quite understand
The worth of a soul and the change that's wrought
By the touch of a Master's hand."

    Jesus can take a broken life and mend it. He takes a flute that has been crushed and gives it a new song. He breathes life into the dying embers of a person's heart. He restores someone who has strayed and makes him into something beautiful. He takes that which is considered of little value and makes it into something of infinite worth. And that's good news!

"For I know the plans I have for you," says the Lord. *"They are plans for good and not for evil, to give you a future and a hope."*   Jeremiah 29:11

This song speaks of God's healing love and power.

There is No Chain

*There is no heart too wounded,
There is no heart so broken that He can't mend.
There is no child so lost he can't be found.
There is no life He can't defend.*

*And there is no valley, no pit too low,
For He is much deeper still.
No life is so hopeless, no heart so empty
That Jesus can't fill.*

*There is no place that He cannot reach,
No hurt that He cannot see.
No matter where you cry out to Him,
There is nowhere that He can't be.*

*He is here waiting, arms open wide.
Just surrender to His will.
No need to be empty, hungry or thirsty;
Jesus can fill.*

*And there's no chain that can't be broken,
There is no pain that He can't feel.
There's no life that can't be rescued,
There's no wound too deep to heal.*

*There's no mountain He can't conquer,
There is no storm that He can't still.
There's no foe that can defeat Him.
But is there a heart that He can't fill?*

*There is one heart that Jesus can't fill,
A heart that won't let Him in.
But if you will let Him,
Jesus will fill you again and again.*

*You are my Father, I am Your child.
There is no better place to me
Than to surrender to Your loving arms
Wherever I may be.*

*And there is no darkness, no barren place,
No desert too low or high,
To keep me from drinking right from the well
That never runs dry.*

Written by Dennis Jernigan. From the album "Daddy's Song," Shepherd's Music, 1992.

11
For Those Who are Successful

Success: The achievement of something desired, planned, or attempted. The gaining of fame or prosperity.

> *"What good will it be for a man if he gains the whole world, yet forfeits his soul?"*
> Matthew 16:26

He had everything a man could want — fame, wealth, a large family, a position of honor and prestige. People came from distant lands to seek his counsel. He was an author and composer, an administrator and architect, a diplomat and businessman. He was called the wisest man who ever lived. Yet somewhere along the way King Solomon lost sight of the eternal goal. His life slowly but surely eroded, and in later years he wrote these words:

"I denied myself nothing my eyes desired; I refused my heart no pleasure. My heart took delight in all my work, and this was the reward for all my labor. Yet when I surveyed all that my *hands had done and what I had toiled to achieve, everything was meaningless, a chasing after the wind..."* Ecclesiastes 2:10,11

Perhaps, like Solomon, your life is going very well. You have already achieved more than you thought possible. Yet peace and contentment elude you. If you stop the hectic pace long enough to sit and reflect, and are completely honest with yourself, you may wonder, along with the author of a well known song, "Is that all there is?" There is a longing within you that is unfulfilled, and all the treasure on earth won't fill that void. King Solomon said that God has *"set eternity in the hearts of men"* (Ecclesiastes 3:11). We are created in the image of God, and only He can satisfy that inner longing.

Solomon also wrote to those who think they will choose God later in life:

"Remember your creator in the days of your youth, before the days of trouble come and the years approach when you will say, 'I find no pleasure in them.' " Ecclesiastes 12:1

God Helps Those Who Help Themselves?

This familiar quotation sounds so biblical, but I'm told it is actually from the pen of Ben Franklin. It echoed my philosophy in years past, since self-sufficiency was an important part of my credo. I believed that I could accomplish almost anything if I worked hard and used my resources well. I believed there was a God, but didn't think I really needed Him, except in dire emergencies. I certainly wouldn't bother Him with seemingly small matters since He had serious prayer requests to answer and the whole universe to run.

I smile now at the arrogance of that viewpoint. Imagine thinking that I could handle things better than He, or that God the Almighty, the God of the universe might get His circuits overloaded if one more request came His way!

Giving our hearts to Christ does not mean that we become mindless robots. I am convinced that God expects us to use the intellect and talents He's given us and to benefit from our education and life experiences. In fact, Jesus calls to task those who do not use their gifts.[1]

By all means utilize the resources God has given you; work hard and achieve. We, our families, and society all benefit from the fruit of such labor. But allow yourself to receive untold blessings as you seek *His will* and walk in the path He chose for you even before you were born. Talk to Him every day and submit your plans, hopes, dreams, and needs to Him. His Word says:

"Commit to the Lord whatever you do, and your plans will succeed."   Proverbs 16:3

God does not object to wealth, fame, or possessions, but our heart attitude toward these things is significant. We need to keep a balance, remember that life is short, and never lose sight of the end goal, eternal life with God.

In his book, *And The Angels Were Silent*,[2] Max Lucado compares a child building a sand castle on the beach with a man working feverishly to build an empire of fame and wealth in his lifetime. He says they are both builders of castles, and for both the tide will rise and the end will come. But the child sees it coming and is prepared for its inevitability. The adult becomes terrified as the waves of the years attack his work, and he attempts to defend it at all costs. The author says,

"You've seen people treat this world like it was a permanent home. It's not. You've seen people pour time and energy into life like it will last forever. It won't.... We are all in transit. Someday the plane will stop and the de-boarding will begin. Wise are those who are ready when the pilot says to get off.... I don't know much about sand castles, but children do. Watch them and learn. Go ahead and build, but build with a child's heart. When the sun sets and the tides take – applaud. Salute the process of life, take your father's hand, and go home."

Endnotes

[1] Matthew 25:14-29
[2] Lucado, Max, *And The Angels Were Silent* (New York: Walker and Co., 1993) p. 137.

Christ offers to men what other religions cannot. Let me illustrate by a man who cannot swim being cast into a lake.

What is the best word Confucius has for the man who is sinking? "Profit by your experience."

What is the most hopeful message Buddha has for him? "Struggle."

What is the most encouraging teaching of Hinduism for the sinking man? "You may have another opportunity in the next incarnation."

And what does Jesus Christ say?
"Take my hand."

John R. Mott

12
What is More Precious than Gold?

Worth: The quality that renders something desirable, useful, or valuable.

"For I know the plans I have for you," declares the Lord, "plans to prosper you and not to harm you, plans to give you a hope and a future. Then you will call upon me and come and pray to me, and I will listen to you. You will seek me and find me when you seek me with all your heart."
Jeremiah 29:11

He had grown accustomed to the adulation of the crowd and relished it. His athletic talent was apparent even in childhood, and now, as a young adult, Jim's dream of being a professional ball player had come true. He basked in the applause, money and fame.

Yet in one shattering moment his whole world came crashing down. Jim suffered a disabling injury and would never play competitive sports again. At the age of 24 his life seemed finished.

If he wasn't a star athlete, who was he? That ability had been his source of identity and self worth most of his life. He felt washed up, useless, hopeless.

Jim and countless others are haunted by a prevailing societal philosophy that equates one's value with what he owns or can create. This view is rooted in existentialism, a school of thought that denies the existence of God, and believes man is responsible personally only to himself. He is isolated in an indifferent universe and cannot find anything or anyone else to depend upon. This viewpoint holds that a person does not have inherent worth as a human being; rather, his value is calculated on what he has achieved and what he can produce. Everything is permitted if there is no accountability to God and no eternal life.

Can you see how this influences our value system? If there is no Divine Creator then one's existence is unexplainable, mere random chance. If one is not a unique, specially created individual with an everlasting future, then it follows that man has little intrinsic value. He is worth only what he possesses or creates here and now.

Society itself is threatened by the broader issue of personal responsibility. If anything is permitted, if one has no eternal destiny, no obligation to God or to others, then what's wrong with stealing, perversion, cheating? The prevailing philosophy says 'if it feels good, do it',

Or 'do whatever it takes' to succeed, including stepping on anyone in your way.

From this viewpoint, your worth is not based on your inherent value as a human being created in God's image. Instead you are judged on what you can produce. In society's view, you are valuable if you are attractive or wealthy, young or athletically gifted, or have letters next to your name such as Dr. or Ph.D. What happens if you are none of the above, or if you become old, ill, or poor? Society would brand you as one of little worth.

Fortunately, this is not the way God sees you. Jesus ministered to rich and poor alike, to the downtrodden as well as those in positions of power. Why? Because of the infinite intrinsic worth of each person.

You have a purpose and a destiny. You are more precious than gold, not because of who you are, but because of Whose you are. You are worthwhile not because of what you produce, how you look or what you have, but because you are God's workmanship, created in His image and likeness. Your destiny is eternal life with Him in heaven. His Word tells how He feels about you.

"The Lord your God is with you.... He will take great delight in you, he will quiet you with his love, he will rejoice over you with singing."
Zephaniah 3:17

There is so much more to be written in your story. There are songs to be sung, tales to be told, mountains to climb, life to live. The best is yet to come! Enjoy the journey, but in all your decisions remember what is really important. Keep your eye fixed on the goal, eternal life with Christ. God doesn't want to hinder you, rather He wants you to be all you were created to be. What He has planned for you is better than anything you could imagine.

The next time you are in a lonely place, or overwhelmed by circumstances, or wondering what life is all about and hungering for something more, call on Jesus. He's been waiting to hear from you. When He went home to Heaven, He left the door open. God loves you with an everlasting love and wants to give you blessings untold.

My prayer is that you will know the hope and peace of life in Christ. May you be blessed with a joyful journey.

We are both on a pilgrimage, and our lives will go on after we leave this earth. By the grace of God, I know where I'll spend eternity. I plan to be in heaven with the Lord forever, and I want you there with me. *Be there! Please, be there!*

"No eye has seen, no ear has heard, no mind has conceived what God has prepared for those who love him..."   1 Corinthians 2:9

Those who are in Christ never have to worry about seeing each other for the last time.

Epilogue

For You Who Have Asked Christ into Your Heart

Next Steps – Growing

Grow: To develop and reach maturity, thrive. to become by a gradual process or by degrees

"When someone becomes a Christian he becomes a brand new person inside. He is not the same any more. A new life has begun!"
2Corinthians 5:17, LB

Three-year-old Jordyn delighted in the story about a caterpillar becoming a butterfly. The new creature experienced a lot of changes, and it took awhile to get used to them. He wasn't crawling on the ground anymore. He had wings now, and had to learn to use them. It was a good feeling, but probably a little strange. He didn't live the way he formerly did, and had to become familiar with new experiences and a different way of looking at things. His whole perspective on life changed.

Like that butterfly, a new Christian gradually undergoes a transformation. If you have received Christ into your heart, you've begun a whole new life. You are a participant in God's covenant, with all of its privileges and duties. When you enter a new realm, whether it's marriage, a new job, or going to college, there are guidelines that help you to grow and prosper in that endeavor.

So it is with your new life in Christ. Here are some steps that will help you to mature in this sphere.

Communicate with God. Talk to Him every day. You would not go days or weeks on end in silence at home or on the job; so too in this new relationship you need to converse with the Lord. Prayer is simply a conversation with Him, in your own words and own way. It is also listening to God as He communicates in that "still small voice" within you. You will grow in your ability to speak and listen to the Lord as you practice daily.

Read the owner's manual, just as you would study a corporate or college handbook that gives you guidelines for success in that institution. Our manual is the Bible, which has written directions to pilot us through life.

Attend in-service education. In the workplace there are classes or programs to update our skills and knowledge. The comparable lessons in the Christian life can be learned by attending a Bible- believing church regularly. It is also very helpful to participate in Sunday school or a Bible study if one is available.

Fellowship. My family members belong to groups that reflect their careers or interests, such as The American Chemical Society, The American Rose Society, or The Air Force Association. For Christians, it is beneficial to become associated with others who believe as you do. They can encourage you and help you to grow in this new life. A good place to meet such people is at church.

A note of caution: Beware of false cults that masquerade as Christian organizations and claim to stand on scriptural truth. Some of their characteristics include denying that Jesus is God and is equal to the Father, emphasizing salvation by works rather than through God's grace, having a book other than the Bible as its center, or overly emphasizing a person, leader, or founder other than Christ.

Guard Your Heart. In this multimedia age with it's graphic portrayal of violence and perversion, we need to be careful about what we watch, listen to, and read. Take care what you let enter into your mind and spirit, and your home. The Bible says:
 " Keep and guard your heart with all vigilance and above all that you guard, for out of it flow the springs of life"   Proverbs 5:24 Amplified

Trust God to help you grow. A loving parent is delighted to see progress in his child and will do everything possible to help him mature. God knows the pitfalls ahead of time and will guide you in avoiding them. He will also steer you in the right direction if you will listen. Remember, God delights in you and *wants* to bless you.

"I will instruct you and teach you in the way you should go; I will counsel you and watch over you." Psalm 32:8

The Manufacturer's Handbook

Handbook: A concise manual or reference book providing specific information or instruction about a subject.

Bible: The sacred book of Christianity, a collection of ancient writings including the books of both the Old Testament and the New Testament.

"The whole Bible was given to us by inspiration from God and is useful to teach us what is true and to make us realize what is wrong in our lives; it straightens us out and helps us to do what is right. It is God's way of making us well prepared at every point..."
                              2 Timothy 3:16,17, LB

The Bible has been called "The Manufacturer's Handbook." Like the set of directions that come with an appliance, a car, or a piece of equipment we purchase, Scripture contains a set of directions from the Creator on how to keep ourselves in good working order.

Why read the Bible?
- The Bible is not just a collection of facts. It is a Book of life, a letter from God, your Creator, to you.
- Scripture is God's way of communicating with us. It is His autobiography, revealing His character, His ways, and His purpose for us and for mankind.
- It has the answers we need. It gives guidance in every area of existence. As Grandpa Nehmsmann used to say, "When all else fails, read the directions!"

How Do I know the Bible is the Word of God?

- *Harmony of the Bible*

  It was written over a time span of 1500 years by over 40 authors from every walk of life. Writers include kings (David and Solomon), herdsmen (Moses and Amos), fishermen (Peter and John), a rabbi (Paul), and a physician (Luke).

  Scripture was penned on three different continents (Asia, Africa, and Europe) and in three languages (Hebrew, Greek, and Aramaic). *Yet it all flows together as a whole, telling us about God's faithfulness, character, commandments, and promises.*

- *Fulfillment of prophecies*

    The Old Testament contains numerous prophecies about the birth of Christ that are fulfilled in the New Testament in the life, death, and resurrection of Jesus.

    For those of you with an analytical mindset, there are 25 specific predictions in the Old Testament about the life and death of Christ that have already been fulfilled. These were written over a time span of 500 years, from 1000 BC to 500 BC, by different prophets, yet they were all literally fulfilled in one person, Jesus Christ. The statistical probability of that happening is 1 in 33,554,432. There are 109 predictions about Christ's birth that were literally fulfilled. Apply the law of compound probabilities to this and the chances are one in billions that these would be fulfilled in one person.

- *Archeological evidence*

    There have been numerous archeological discoveries in recent years that validate the authenticity of Scripture. Perhaps the best known are The Dead Sea Scrolls, dating back to 200 BC - 70 AD. These were found in 1947-1952 in a cave near Jericho. They haven't all been deciphered yet, but so far we know they contain fragments from nearly all Old Testament books, as well as shedding light on the New Testament.

Reasons people don't read the Bible:

- *Some say it is too difficult to understand.*

   For easier comprehension and study you might want to obtain a modern translation of the Bible, such as the New International Version, The Living Bible, or The New King James Version. The Bible was written for us, and if we approach it with a desire to learn, we will find it quite comprehensible.

- *People go by what others say about the Bible*

   You may have heard negative comments about Scripture, but in all fairness, before you condemn it, read it first. Don't let other people tell you what God's Word says, even if they are preachers. Read it for yourself. I challenge you to read the Bible through and see if you come away with the same opinion you had before you began. I believe you will be surprised at what the Scripture contains.

How to read the Bible:

- Get a translation you can understand.

- Scripture doesn't necessarily have to be read in order from front to back. Some suggest starting with the Gospel of John in the New Testament, which teaches about the work and person of Jesus Christ. Then one might want to read the other gospels and the rest of the New Testament straight through before going on to the book of Genesis and the Old Testament.

- Set aside a time daily to read Scripture. Read the Bible at your own pace, but read some every day. (It has been said that the entire Bible can be read in less than 80 hours; you then will have read the world's all time best seller!)

"The word that God speaks is alive and full of power – making it active, operative, energizing and effective..."   Hebrews 4:12, Amplified

We search the world
for truth;
We cull the good, the pure,
the beautiful,
From all old flower fields
of the soul;
And, weary seekers of
the best,
We come back laden from
our quest,
To find that all the
sages said
Is in the Book
our mothers read.

John Greenleaf Whittier

Becoming A New Creation

As you try to live according to God's plan, the old way of life will exert some force, but this pull will get weaker as you grow stronger in the Lord. You may make mistakes along the way, but that is part of growing. I never stop loving my children, even if they miss the mark occasionally. God feels the same way about you; tell Him you're sorry and pick yourself up and move on.

Don't let your faith be ruled by emotions. There may be days when you don't feel saved, redeemed, or loved by God. Life can be especially challenging when you are weary or stressed. Rather than allowing your feelings to dictate your perception of truth, rely on God's word in Scripture.

Be patient with yourself. When a seed is planted, it takes time to grow. As you nurture that seed with prayer, obedience to God's word, and fellowship with other believers, you will soon be amazed at how far you've come.

There are numerous resources to help you live as a new creation. The most important is the Lord. He *wants* you to succeed in this new life.

Christian bookstores have many good books on prayer, how to grow in Christ, and how to study the Bible. Attending a Bible-based church.

Sunday school, or Bible study is very beneficial. Christian friends will *want* to assist you.

I pray regularly for all of you who read this book that God will help you to know Him better and that:

"The Lord bless you, and watch, guard and keep you; the Lord make His face to shine upon and enlighten you and be gracious (kind, merciful and giving favor) to you; the Lord lift up His countenance upon you and give you peace [tranquillity of heart and life continually]."

Numbers 6:24-26, Amplified

Promises from Scripture

"Jehovah Himself is caring for you! He is your defender. He protects you day and night. He keeps you from all evil, and preserves your life. He keeps his eye upon you as you come and go, and always guards you." Psalm 121:5-8

"God who began the good work within you will keep right on helping you grow in his grace..."
Phillipians 1:6

"With God, everything is possible" Matthew 19:26

"I [God] have loved you, O My people, with an everlasting love; with loving-kindness I have drawn you to Me." Jeremiah 31:3

"Surely you have a wonderful future ahead of you. There is hope for you yet!" Proverbs 23:18

"Don't be afraid, for I [God] have ransomed you; I have called you by name; you are Mine. When you go through deep waters and great difficulty, you will not drown! When you walk through the fire of oppression, you will not be burned up – the flames

will not consume you. For I am the Lord your God, your Savior..." Isaiah 43:1-3

"God is faithful to His word and to His compassionate nature, and He can be trusted not to let you be tempted and tried...beyond your ability and strength...and power to endure, but with the temptation He will always also provide the way out – the means of escape to a landing place – that you may be capable and strong and powerful patiently to bear up under it."
1 Corinthians 10:13, Amplified

"Be strong and courageous. Do not be terrified; do not be discouraged, for the Lord your God is with you wherever you go." Joshua 1:9, NIV

"He [God] forgives all my sins. He heals me. He ransoms me from hell. He surrounds me with loving-kindness and tender mercies. He fills my life with good things! My youth is renewed like the eagle's! " Psalm 103:3-5

"Surely goodness and mercy shall follow me all the days of my life; and I will dwell in the house of the Lord forever." Psalm 23:6, KJV

Scripture quotations are taken from The Living Bible, unless otherwise noted.

About the Author

Camille Nehmsmann, a registered nurse, received her diploma from St. Peter's School of Nursing in New Brunswick, NJ and her degree in school nursing from Glassboro State College, now called Rowan College, in Glassboro, NJ. She worked briefly in hospital nursing before her children were born.

Camille received Christ into her heart in 1977, and since then has participated in a number of intercessory prayer groups and taught on the power of intercessory prayer. She has also led home fellowship groups and been active in women's ministries.

Camile has written three other books whose purpose is to lead people into a closer walk with the Lord.

Camille and her husband Lou have been married 40 years and have three children and three grandchildren. They presently reside in Washington Township, PA.

Additional copies available from:

Good News Ministries
301 Young Drive
Apollo, Pa. 15613

Also available from the same author:

Discover Hidden Treasure, a brief summary of every book of the Bible including a chronology of the old Testament and historical backgrounds to Biblical events. Written in a simple easily understood way with encouraging promises from God's Word.

Safe In The Secret Place, a verse by verse study of Psalm 91, with dramatic stories of how God intervened to rescue people from challenging situations. Learn about the ministry of angels, how to overcome fear, and how to have a closer walk with God.

The Power of Intercessory Prayer, a simple step by step guide to intercession, including faith building stories of dramatic answers to prayer. Some of the topics discussed in this book are spiritual warfare, the importance of praise, scripture praying, interceding for the unsaved, and group prayer.

To begin new life in Christ you can say this prayer or a similar one in your own words:

Lord Jesus Christ, I admit that I am a sinner and that You died and rose again to redeem me from my sins. Please forgive me. Come into my heart and be my Lord and Savior. Thank You, God, that You have heard my prayer and I am now in Your kingdom. Help me to live the life You have chosen for me. Amen!

If you said that prayer with your heart, Jesus assures you that you are saved from hell and can look forward to eternity in heaven as well as abundant life here on earth. Welcome to life in a new dimension!

To Order books write to:

Camille Nehmsmann
301 Young Drive
Apollo, Pa. 15613

Safe In The Secret Place -------------- $8.95
                                   3 for $25.00
Meet The God Who Loves You ----- $6.95
Discover Hidden Treasure ----------- $5.95
The Power of Intercessory Prayer -$6.95

20% discount for orders of 20 or more

Add $2.00 for postage for the first book,
and 50 cents postage for each additional book.

Make checks payable to Camille Nehmsmann

Book Title	Number of Copies	Price
_____	_____	_____
_____	_____	_____
_____	_____	_____
_____	Postage	_____
	Total	_____

Mail to: (Please Print Clearly)

Name:_____

Address:_____

City:_____

State:_____ Zip:_____